W9-ARJ-435

GROWING UP

My First Day at a New School

Charlotte Guillain

Heinemann Library
Chicago, Illinois

www.heinemannraintree.com
Visit our website to find out more information about Heinemann-Raintree books.

To order:

☎ Phone 888-454-2279

💻 Visit www.heinemannraintree.com to browse our catalog and order online.

© 2011 Heinemann Library
an imprint of Capstone Global Library, LLC
Chicago, Illinois

All rights reserved. No part of this publication may be reproduced or transmitted in any form or by any means, electronic or mechanical, including photocopying, recording, taping, or any information storage and retrieval system, without permission in writing from the publisher.

Edited by Dan Nunn, Rebecca Rissman, and Sian Smith
Designed by Joanna Hinton-Malivoire
Picture research by Elizabeth Alexander
Originated by Capstone Global Library Ltd
Printed in the United States of America by
  Worzalla Publishing.

15 14 13 12 11 10
10 9 8 7 6 5 4 3 2 1

Library of Congress Cataloging-in-Publication Data
Guillain, Charlotte.
  My first day at a new school / Charlotte Guillain.
     p. cm. — (Growing up)
  Includes bibliographical references and index.
  ISBN 978-1-4329-4796-5 (hc)—ISBN 978-1-4329-4806-1 (pb) 1. First day of school—Juvenile literature. I. Title.
  LB1556.G85 2011
  371.002—dc22   2010024189

Acknowledgments
We would like to thank the following for permission to reproduce photographs: Alamy pp. 15 (© Cultura), 19 (© Paul Doyle), 23 glossary assembly (© Enigma); Corbis pp. 10 (© Creasource), 12 (© JGI/Jamie Grill/Blend Images); Getty Images pp. 4 (Woods Wheatcroft/Aurora), 5 (DAJ), 11 (Yellow Dog Productions/Lifesize); Photolibrary pp. 7 (Comstock), 8 (Chevalier Virginie/Oredia), 13 (Monkey Business Images Ltd/Stockbroker), 16 (Stuart Pearce/age footstock), 17 (Jose Luis Pelaez Inc/Blend Images), 18 (Lemoine Lemoine/BSIP Medical), 20 (Picture Partners/age footstock), 21 (Chevalier Virginie/Oredia), 23 glossary exercise (Jose Luis Pelaez Inc/Blend Images), 23 glossary attendance (Monkey Business Images Ltd/Stockbroker); Shutterstock pp. 6 (© Sandra Gligorijevic), 9 (© Morgan Lane Photography), 14 (© sovisdesign).

Front cover photograph of students in class volunteering reproduced with permission of Photolibrary (Monkey Business Images Ltd/Stockbroker). Back cover photographs of bags reproduced with permission of Shutterstock (© Sandra Gligorijevic), and a bus reproduced with permission of Shutterstock (© Morgan Lane Photography).

Every effort has been made to contact copyright holders of material reproduced in this book. Any omissions will be rectified in subsequent printings if notice is given to the publisher.

Disclaimer
All the Internet addresses (URLs) given in this book were valid at the time of going to press. However, due to the dynamic nature of the Internet, some addresses may have changed or ceased to exist since publication. While the author and publisher regret any inconvenience this may cause readers, no responsibility for any such changes can be accepted by either the author or the publisher.

Contents

When Will I Start at a New School?. 4

What Do I Need to Take to School? 6

How Do I Get to School?. 8

What Happens When I Get to School? 10

What Happens in My Classroom? 12

What Do I Need to Know?. 14

What Will Happen During the Day? 16

Is It OK to Be Nervous? 18

What Happens at the End of the Day? 20

Do's and Don'ts at School 22

Picture Glossary. 23

Find Out More 24

Index 24

Some words are shown in bold, **like this**.
You can find them in the glossary on page 23.

When Will I Start at a New School?

All children have a first day at school.

Most children start school for the first time when they have finished nursery school or preschool.

Older children also sometimes start at a new school.

If you move or go to a middle school, then you will go to a new school.

What Do I Need to Take to School?

When you go to school, you will need to take a coat if the weather is cold or wet.

You will also need a bag to carry books and homework to and from school.

You might need to take a packed lunch, unless you are having school lunches.

You do not need to take toys to school, since everything you need will be in your classroom.

How Do I Get to School?

If you live near your school, you may walk to school with an adult.

Walking to school is a good way to get **exercise** in the morning.

If you live farther away, you might need to ride on a school bus.

Some children travel to school by car.

What Happens When I Get to School?

When you get to school, you will see lots of other children on the playground.

The teachers will open the door when it is time to go in.

Everyone goes into school and finds their own cubby or locker.

When you have put away your things, you can go into your new classroom.

What Happens in My Classroom?

All schools start the day in different ways.

In many schools, your teacher will meet you as you come into the classroom.

You might start the day by sitting down together and greeting each other.

Your teacher will probably check that everyone is there by taking **attendance**.

What Do I Need to Know?

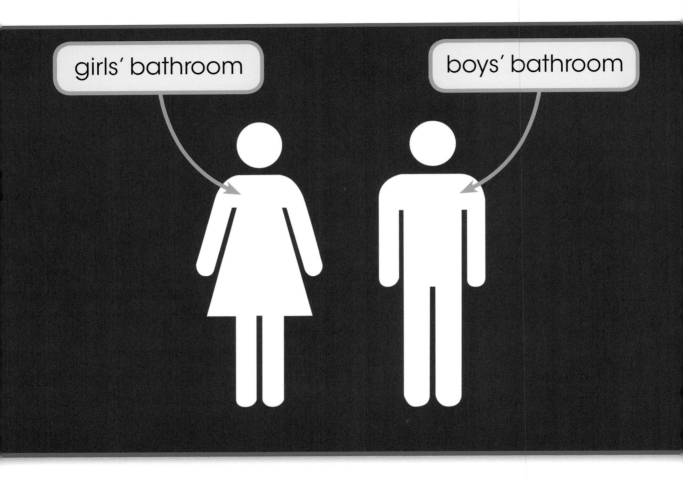

It is important to know your way around your new school.

You need to know where the bathrooms and your cubby or locker are.

You also need to know the names of the teachers and where your classroom is.

Don't be afraid to ask for help if you are not sure about anything.

What Will Happen During the Day?

The school day will be different in all schools.

You will get to know the other children as you work and play together.

Many schools have snack time, lunch time, and play time during the day.

There might be an **assembly** with the rest of the school or some other classes.

Is It OK to Be Nervous?

Most children feel nervous when they start a new school for the first time.

There will be other children who feel the same as you.

Tell your teacher if you feel unhappy.

He or she will help you make friends and find something to do that you enjoy.

What Happens at the End of the Day?

At the end of the day, your class might gather to say goodbye.

Then you will need to collect all of your things before leaving the classroom.

Sometimes children go home on a school bus.

Others are met by their parents or another caregiver.

Dos and Don'ts at School

Dos:

✓ Do listen carefully and quietly to your teacher.

✓ Do raise your hand when you want to speak.

✓ Do be kind to other children.

✓ Do have fun!

Don'ts:

✗ Don't run in the school building.

✗ Don't be afraid to ask if you are not sure about anything.

✗ Don't forget to try your best.

Picture Glossary

 **assembly** meeting for everyone in school

 **attendance** check of students in the classroom that the teacher does at the start of the day

 **exercise** type of sport or activity. Running and walking are good ways to get some exercise.

Find Out More

Books

Child, Lauren. *I Am Too Absolutely Small for School*. Cambridge, Mass.: Candlewick, 2005.

Joyce, Melanie. *First Day at School* (Fred Bear and Friends). Pleasantville, N.Y.: Weekly Reader, 2008.

Websites

Learn more about what to expect on your first day at a new school: **http://kidshealth.org/kid/feeling/school/back_to_school.html**

Index

assembly 17
attendance 13
bag 6
bathroom 14
books 6
children 4–5, 9, 10, 16, 18, 21
class 17, 20
classroom 7, 11, 12, 15, 20

cubby 11, 14
friends 19
locker 11, 14
nervous 18
packed lunch 7
playground 10
school bus 9, 21
school lunch 7
teacher 10, 12–13, 15, 19, 22